Meeting Legal Needs?

Meeting Legal Needs?

An evaluation of a scheme for personal injury victims

HAZEL GENN

SSRC Centre for Socio-Legal Studies
Wolfson College, Oxford.

SSRC Centre for Socio-Legal Studies, Oxford
Greater Manchester Legal Services Committee

SSRC Centre for Socio-Legal Studies, Oxford
Greater Manchester Legal Services Committee

Published by SSRC Centre for Socio-Legal Studies
ISBN 0 86226 044 2

This research was supported by a grant from the Nuffield Foundation.

Contents

Foreword

This report was commissioned by the Greater Manchester Legal Services Committee which was formed in 1977 as an experiment in the greater involvement of lay people in the administration of legal services. The aims of the Committee are to monitor, extend and improve legal services in Greater Manchester. It consists of 10 lawyers and 15 lay persons who represent a wide range of organisations and interests throughout the area.

In furtherance of these aims, over the past four years the Committee has undertaken many projects, some of which have led to the legal profession taking its own initiative to extend and improve legal services, whilst others have been directly organised and controlled by the Committee itself.

Arising from the Report of the Pearson Commission and the research in the area of Compensation for Personal Injury conducted by the SSRC Centre for Socio-Legal Studies at Oxford, the Committee expressed concern about the large number of persons who sustained accidents but did not seek any kind of legal advice about the possibility of claiming compensation. This was further emphasized at the Seminar on the Unmet Need for Legal Services which the Committee held in 1978, when it was demonstrated that one of the main reasons why persons who had sustained accidents did not consult a solicitor, was the fear of the cost of doing so.

To meet this need and try to overcome these fears, the Committee decided to publish a leaflet which would not only give advice to anyone sustaining an accident in the street, at home or at work about claiming compensation, but also give some positive assistance by offering an initial interview with a solicitor free of charge. This was only done with the full co-operation of the solicitors in the area who gave their overwhelming support to the idea. With the assistance of the Lord Chancellor's Department and the Central Office of Information, the leaflet was first published in March 1978 with an accompanying poster advertising it. The first print of 20,000 was distributed to hospitals, public libraries, Citizens' Advice Bureaux and the many agencies which give advice to the public and, where necessary, refer them to solicitors.

A further 10,000 have since been printed and distributed and the leaflet has also been translated into Bengali, Gujarati, Hindi, Punjabi and Urdu.

The following report analyses the results of the first 21 months of the operation of the scheme and comments on its effectiveness. The Committee are most grateful to Hazel Genn, who has personally carried out all the detailed work and research which has led to her report. The Committee would also like to thank the SSRC Centre for Socio-Legal Studies for their assistance and co-operation, and to the Nuffield Foundation without whose grant the research would not have been possible.

Eric Knott
Secretary
Greater Manchester Legal Services Committee

Preface

Despite concern expressed both before and since the Report of the Pearson Commission about the difficulties facing accident victims seeking to obtain compensation for injuries through the tort system, there seems to be no evidence that any substantial changes in the present system are planned. Whatever the merits or disadvantages of a fault-based system of compensation for personal injury, it is likely to be with us for the immediate, and probably the not so immediate future. Given this likelihood, and what is now known of the factors which constrain accident victims from seeking legal advice and pursuing claims for damages, an experiment designed to ameliorate some of the shortcomings of the system must be regarded as timely, both by those who might benefit directly from the scheme and those interested in improving the quality of legal services generally.

This report represents an evaluation of the Manchester Accident Leaflet Scheme based primarily on information obtained directly from those accident victims who made use of the scheme during the first 21 months of its operation. Any research involving the collection of survey data produces a great deal of paperwork which requires careful guarding and organization. I am grateful to Sheila Goodman in Manchester for her help in this respect and for dealing with telephone enquiries. I would also like to thank Trisha Powell for her assistance in the administration of the survey and organization of the data; Sally Lloyd-Bostock, Daniel Appleby, and Donald Harris for constructive criticism of drafts; and Noël Harris for conscientious typing and re-typing of the final manuscript.

Hazel Genn
Oxford

1

Introduction: The 'Legal Needs' of Accident Victims

There appears to be a broad agreement among legal writers and those involved in the delivery of legal services, that despite the size of the legal profession and the existence of the Legal Aid Scheme, there is nonetheless a need for legal services which is at present inadequately met. Although there are difficulties in defining the range of problems which might give rise to specifically 'legal' needs as opposed to other kinds of needs, the Royal Commission on Legal Services suggested in 1979 that:

> "however restricted is the definition of need for legal services, such services are, in some areas and for certain classes of society, seriously inadequate."[1]

Few people would assert that all problems which involve the infringement of legal rights are necessarily best solved by resorting to litigation. There are, however, situations in which legal action may represent the only prospect for an individual of securing a satisfactory solution to his problem, and where failure to seek legal advice results in unnecessary hardship. Accidental injury causes suffering and financial loss for hundreds of thousands of people every year. Although some compensation for loss of earnings is available for certain categories of accident victims through the workings of the social security system, for many who suffer accidental injury, the only possible means of obtaining compensation may be by bringing a claim in tort against a negligent third-party. The responsibility for initiating such an action lies with the injured plaintiff and failure to do so means he must fall back on any entitlement to sick pay or social security - or on nothing.

1 FAILURE TO SEEK LEGAL ADVICE

Legal commentators and practising lawyers have, in the past, subscribed to the view that only a small proportion of potential claims for damages arising from personal injury are actually brought by accident victims. This speculation has recently been confirmed and expanded by two important sources. First, the Royal Commission on Civil Liability and Compensation for Personal Injury (hereafter referred to as the Pearson Commission) reported in 1978, on the basis of its own commissioned survey, that only about *6 ½ per cent* of all people suffering accidental injury actually obtained any compensation through the tort system.[2] A more recent and comprehensive national survey of compensation and support for victims of illness and injury conducted by the Centre for Socio-Legal Studies in Oxford (hereafter referred to as the National Compensation Survey) found that only *12 per cent* of all *seriously* injured accident victims obtained damages through the tort system.[3] This study looked in detail at the ways in which accident victims came to initiate claims for damages and also at their reasons for failing to do so. The National Compensation Survey findings showed that only *one-quarter* of seriously injured accident victims even considered the possibility of claiming damages, and that of this small minority, only a little over half (56%) actually sought legal advice about the possibility of claiming damages.

Information from these two studies has therefore established unambiguously that victims of accidental injury do not, on the whole, benefit from the tort system of compensation; and that this failure stems as much from failure to seek legal advice as from defeat during the negotiation of a claim.

In the aftermath of an accidental injury the responsibility for initiating a claim for damages rests squarely on the shoulders of the injured individual who is unlikely to have had any experience of personal injury litigation, and whose primary concern is with his physical recovery. Unless he has the backing of a Trade Union, the prospect of embarking on a claim for damages, at a time when resources are normally strained, might seem daunting, if considered at all. The Pearson Commission and the National Compensation Survey showed that even in the minority of cases where the possibility of legal action is considered, many accident victims hesitate to seek legal advice for fear of the cost involved, misunderstanding of the law or simply through lack of knowledge of how to begin. Fears of legal costs were understandably common in the light of another of the National Compensation Survey findings, that knowledge of Legal Aid and the Legal Advice Scheme was scant, even among those accident victims who had actually taken the step of consulting a solicitor about a claim for damages.

For the vast majority of accident victims, however, there is no question of 'hesitating' to seek legal advice, because the idea, apparently, *never occurs to them at all.* Although it is clear that consulting a solicitor cannot guarantee that a claim for damages will be taken up and finally succeed, *failure* to seek legal advice normally ensures that an injured victim will not obtain any damages through the tort system.

2 THE ACCIDENT LEAFLET SCHEME

It was concern about this now well-documented failure of accident victims to seek legal advice which led to the establishment of the scheme being administered by the Greater Manchester Legal Services Committee (GMLSC). In essence, the objectives of the scheme are to provide easily accessible information about legal rights in relation to personal injury by distributing leaflets and posters in hospitals, surgeries, Citizens' Advice Bureaux, and other institutions; and to provide one free interview with a solicitor for those people who complete and return a coupon printed on the back of each leaflet. The principle, then, is to remove or help to overcome three apparently major hurdles in the path of accident victims seeking legal advice. These hurdles are as follows:

1 Lack of knowledge about legal rights in relation to accidental injury
2 Fear of legal costs
3 Uncertainty about how to locate a solicitor and apprehension about making the inital approach

The leaflets and posters advertising the scheme can therefore not only stimulate action amongst injured people who have only vaguely considered a legal claim; they can also plant the idea of claiming in the minds of people who have never consciously considered the possibility of claiming before. When a coupon is completed and sent in, the accident victim knows that he will be able to discuss his accident with a solicitor at least once without incurring any cost at all; and finally, since the solicitor allocated to the accident victim will telephone or write to arrange an appointment, there is no need for him to seek out a solicitor or make the first approach. This is important in view of the extent to which many people are shy of going to see a solicitor for the first time.

It is clear from the comments of scheme users that the combination of ignorance about legal rights, fear of costs and the perceived inaccessibility of solicitors do indeed represent a powerful inhibition against seeking legal services:

> "Most working class people have an inbuilt fear of solicitors and legal matters ... I would not have gone to see a solicitor as I was worried about any possible costs I may incur ... I now find myself better off by far due to the scheme"

> "The scheme is really marvellous, especially for people who are nervous when it comes to seeing a solicitor because it breaks the ice when a solicitor is picked for them..."

> "I had no idea what to do or where to go and when I saw the solicitor I was really put at ease and didn't feel at all nervous"

> "It was so easy to fill in the form and send it off, and it helped a lot to have a solicitor contact me to arrange an interview"

> "If I had not sought advice I would have had no other way of reclaiming any loss of earnings or anything else for that matter. I would not have dreamt of going near a solicitor because of the cost which in no possible way could I afford."

3 EVALUATING THE SCHEME

"Is it a success?" or "Does it work?" are questions which are easy to pose and difficult to answer. Success and failure are relative terms and in the context of evaluative research the conclusions reached depend to a large extent on how the criteria of success are formulated and applied. Although the impact or value of the accident leaflet scheme might be assessed from a number of standpoints, we have taken the broad objective of the scheme to be that of helping to meet a previously unsatisfied need for legal services among people who have suffered from accidental injury. In considering the extent to which the scheme appears to meet this objective, this study has focussed on three key questions, the answers to which, it is felt, provide both objective and subjective evidence of the impact of the scheme:

1 Is the scheme being used by those groups of accident victims who have been identified in previous research as unlikely to seek legal advice about claiming compensation?
2 Is the scheme tapping a reservoir of good causes of action?
3 Are users of the scheme glad of its introduction and satisfied with the way it is working?

The subject matter of question 1 is dealt with in Chapter 2 where, in so far as possible, the characteristics of scheme users have been analysed in relation to the findings of the National Compensation Survey. In that survey great attention was paid to identifying which specific subgroups of accident victims failed to seek legal advice after an accident and which appeared to be more likely to seek advice. Since the NCS represents the most up-to-date and comprehensive body of data dealing with the use of legal services by victims of accidental injury, it appeared to be both valid and useful to look at users of the accident leaflet scheme in relation to those findings.

It is clear that the expectations of a client receiving a free interview are likely to be rather different from those of the solicitor granting the interview. While the client may be pleased of the opportunity to discuss his position without incurring any cost, a solicitor cannot be expected to operate on an entirely altruistic basis. He will be looking for a high proportion of interviews where claims can be taken up. Indeed, it might be said that part of the definition of a need for legal services by accident victims depends on the assumption that there are good causes of action, within the law of tort, which are not being pressed. This is the brunt of the second question posed above and is dealt with in detail in Chapter 3.

Chapter 4 concentrates on the third question, which concerns the subjective feelings of scheme users about their solicitors, the advice they received and the operation of the scheme in relation to their needs and expectations. Chapter 5 presents some views expressed by solicitors about the scheme which complement the views of clients and some of the assumptions in Chapter 3.

Although this study does not pretend to cover adequately all of the issues of relevance to the question of meeting legal needs, it is an attempt to indicate the usefulness of adopting a practical approach to the problem; and if the objective of improving access to legal services is considered worthwhile, the study may be deemed to have a more general application to other types of legal problems.

4 RESEARCH DESIGN AND RESPONSE

The study was designed to obtain information by means of postal questionnaire from all people who had made use of the scheme between its inception in March 1979 and December 1980 in order to evaluate the success or impact of the scheme.

From files maintained by the GMLSC two cross-classified indexes were compiled containing (1) the names and addresses of all those people who had returned coupons requesting a free interview under the scheme; and (2) the names and addresses of solicitors to whom coupons had been forwarded. Excluded from the first index were 13 people who had failed to attend the free interview arranged for them; 13 cases with incomplete addresses; 3 cases where the solicitor had written to the GMLSC to advise that the claim would not be taken up; 7 cases which had been directed to other agencies by the solicitor concerned; and 2 cases where the client had moved from the home address given on the coupon.

Postal questionnaires were sent to 483 people who had returned coupons to the GMLSC between March 1979 and December 1980. The initial mailing of questionnaires with covering letter and return envelope was completed in the week ending 11th February 1981. All letters were individually signed and first class postage was used on both the outgoing envelope and on the return envelope. Stamps rather than franking were used since it was considered that this might improve response by making the approach appear more personal. A copy of the postal questionnaire and covering letter appears in Appendix 2.

After about two-and-a-half weeks, when the flow of responses had dropped a reminder was sent to all non-respondents; and then after a further two-and-a-half weeks a second reminder, together with a fresh questionnaire and return envelope was sent by mail.

The response to the postal questionnaire is summarised in Table 1.1 which shows a high response rate. Of the 483 questionnaires mailed only 14 per cent were entirely unproductive, and the number of usable questionnaires (353) represents 78 per cent of the effective sample of 451. The pattern of postal returns and the results of the analysis of non-respondents is presented in Appendix 1.

Table 1.1. Response to the postal questionnaire

Number of questionnaires mailed	483	
Some information received	390	80·7%
Post Office returns	22	4·5%
Refusals	4	·8%
Lost in post	1	·2%
No response at all	66	13.7%
	483	100·0%
Some information received	390	
Usable questionnaires	353	
Exclusions: Respondent dead	4	
Not an accident	8	
Didn't keep appointment	20	

NOTES

1 Royal Commission on Legal Services Final Report, Vol. I, Cmnd 7648, HMSO 1979.

2 Royal Commission on Civil Liability and Compensation for Personal Injury, Cmnd 7054-1, HMSO 1978.

3 D. Harris, M. Maclean, H. Genn, S. Lloyd-Bostock, P. Fenn, P. Corfield and Y. Brittan, *Compensation and Support for Illness and Injury*, Oxford University Press 1982.

2

Profile of scheme users

The initial task in the evaluation of the scheme was to identify the more important characteristics of the accident victims who had found, or were given, leaflets entitling them to a free interview with a solicitor. Information had been obtained in the postal questionnaire about respondents' basic demographic characteristics, such as age, sex, class etc., as well as other important identifying characteristics like type of accident suffered and the seriousness of the injuries sustained. Taken together, all of these characteristics help to build up a picture of the kinds of people being drawn into the scheme. In addition to simply describing scheme users in these terms, however, it was thought useful to compare, where possible, the characteristics of scheme users with data from the National Compensation Survey (NCS) in order to obtain some idea of the extent to which they differed, if at all, from accident victims who had sought legal advice in that survey. In making this comparison it is possible to draw inferences about the extent to which the scheme is succeeding in reaching specific groups of accident victims previously identified as having a low propensity to seek legal advice following an accident.

1 DEMOGRAPHIC CHARACTERISTICS

Sex. Completed leaflet coupons were received by the GMLSC from roughly equal numbers of men and women. Although the figures from completed postal questionnaires show slightly more women than men, this is accounted for by the fact that men were considerably less likely than women to return their postal questionnaires.[1] Figure 2.1 shows that in the National Compensation Survey, women were overall much *less* likely than men to seek legal advice following an accident. In that survey just under three-quarters of people seeking legal advice were men and just over one-quarter were women. On the basis of this comparison, then, the Manchester scheme appears to be drawing in a relatively large number of women who might not normally be expected to obtain legal advice. As it will be seen below this finding is very much bound up with the fact that relatively high numbers of victims of accidents taking place other than on the road or at work appeared to be making use of the Manchester scheme.

Figure 2.1. Comparison of sex of Manchester scheme users with sex of accident victims taking legal advice in National Compensation Survey.

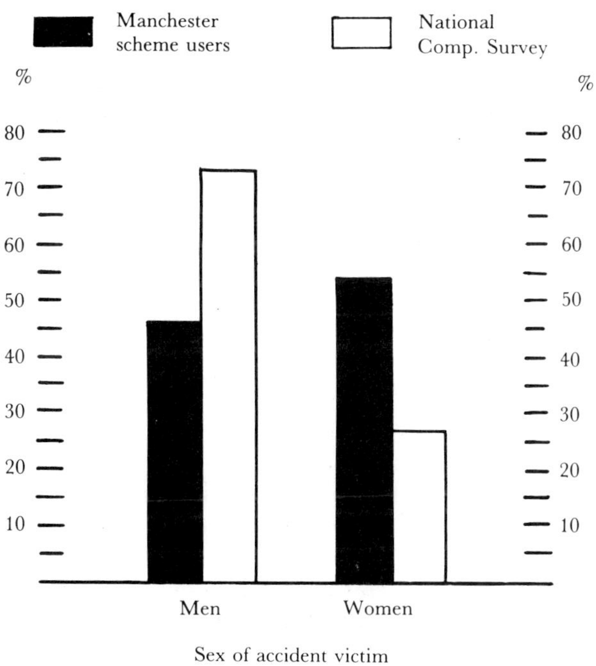

Figure 2.2. Comparison of age group of Manchester scheme users with age group of accident victims taking legal advice in National Compensation Survey.

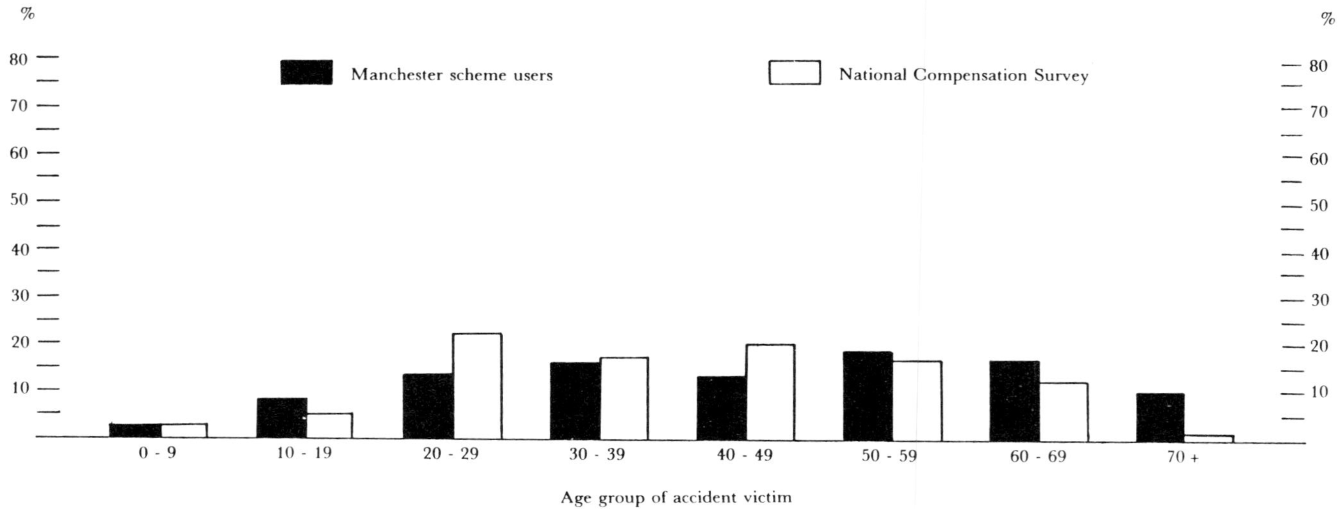

Age. The age distributions shown in Figure 2.2 indicate that scheme users tended on the whole towards the older age categories. More than one-quarter of the people requesting free interviews with solicitors were over the age of 60. This finding again contrasts substantially with the National Compensation Survey in which older age groups suffering accidents were found to be less likely than younger people to seek legal advice. Figure 2.2 shows that the 50 plus age groups represent a consistently higher proportion of scheme users than the proportion of those in the same age groups seeking legal advice in the National Compensation Survey.

Economic Activity. Nearly half of the scheme users were not in any form of employment at the time of completing the postal questionnaire. As one might expect from the age distribution of scheme users some 16 per cent of respondents were retired. A further 10 per cent of users were women not employed outside the home and a relatively high proportion of users were off work as a result of sickness or disability. Some 11 per cent of users were unemployed at the time of completing the questionnaire and there was a small number of users in full-time education (5 cases). Of those people who were in employment, the majority were employed full-time, but this group of full-time workers only represented two-fifths of all people using the scheme. These findings differ considerably from those of the National Compensation Survey in which three-quarters of all claims made for damages were by accident victims who had been in full-time employment at the time of their accident. Figure 2.3 shows the comparison between activity status of scheme users and those seeking legal advice in the National Compensation Survey.

Socio-Economic group. Scheme users were asked to state their occupation or last main paid occupation on the questionnaire and in so far as it was possible from the descriptions given, occupation was categorised according to the Registrar General's Classification of Occupation. In addition, where the scheme user was married the occupation of the spouse was obtained in order to classify the socio-economic grouping of the whole household rather than simply the occupation of the injured scheme user. The somewhat ill-defined categorisation of occupation of scheme users showed that the largest proportion of employed scheme users were

Figure 2.3. Comparison of employment activity of Manchester scheme users with employment activity of accident victims taking legal advice in the National Compensation Survey.[1]

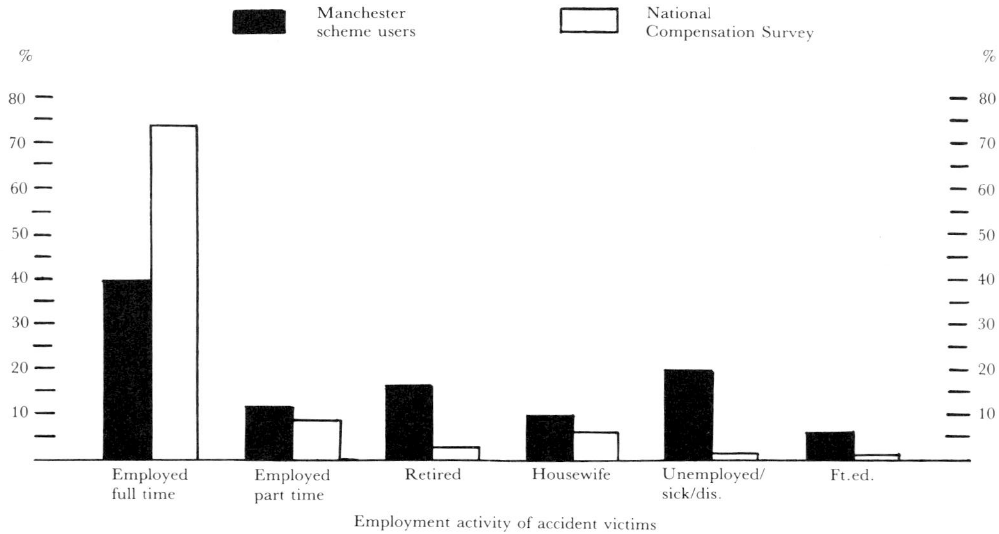

Note

1. These figures are not exactly comparable since the definition of activity status in the Manchester data relates to activity at the time of completing the postal questionnaire, while in the National Compensation Survey the definition related to the time when the accident occurred.

in skilled manual occupations (30 per cent). Just under one-quarter of scheme users were in semi-skilled manual occupations (24 per cent) and routine non-manual workers like clerks, shop assistants etc., were the next largest category (22 per cent). Unskilled manual workers represented 13 per cent of scheme users and professional and managerial groups together represented about 10 per cent of scheme users. In order to compare the socio-economic group of scheme users with that of accident victims seeking legal advice in the National Compensation Survey it was necessary to compare not the occupational group of the person using the scheme, but that of the household, which is conventionally defined on the basis of the occupation of the head of the household. The results of this comparison are shown in Figure 2.4. below. Although the differences are not particularly great there appear to be rather more people using the scheme from professional and managerial households than in the National Compensation Survey as well as rather more in skilled-manual occupations. In general, however, the distribution of scheme users among the six socio-economic groups is roughly the same as that of accident victims seeking legal advice nationally.

2 TYPE OF ACCIDENT SUFFERED

An analysis of the nature of the accidents suffered by users of the Manchester scheme has yielded information which is particularly interesting in the light of the findings of the Pearson Commission and the National Compensation Survey. In both of those studies it was found that accidents occurring anywhere other than on the road or at work very rarely resulted in legal advice being sought. The overwhelming majority of claims for damages among accident victims were found to have been made by people who had suffered road or work accidents. In the Manchester scheme, however, this was by no means the case. Some 38 per cent of scheme users had suffered their accidents either at home, at leisure, in the street or in shops, while 34 per cent had suffered work accidents and 27 per cent had been involved in road accidents either as drivers, passengers or pedestrians. Figure 2.5 shows the very pronounced differences in type of accident suffered by those seeking legal advice in the NCS as compared with type of accident suffered by Manchester scheme users. In the NCS only

Figure 2.4. Comparison of socio-economic group of head of household of Manchester scheme users with socio-economic group of head of household of accident victims taking legal advice in National Compensation Survey.

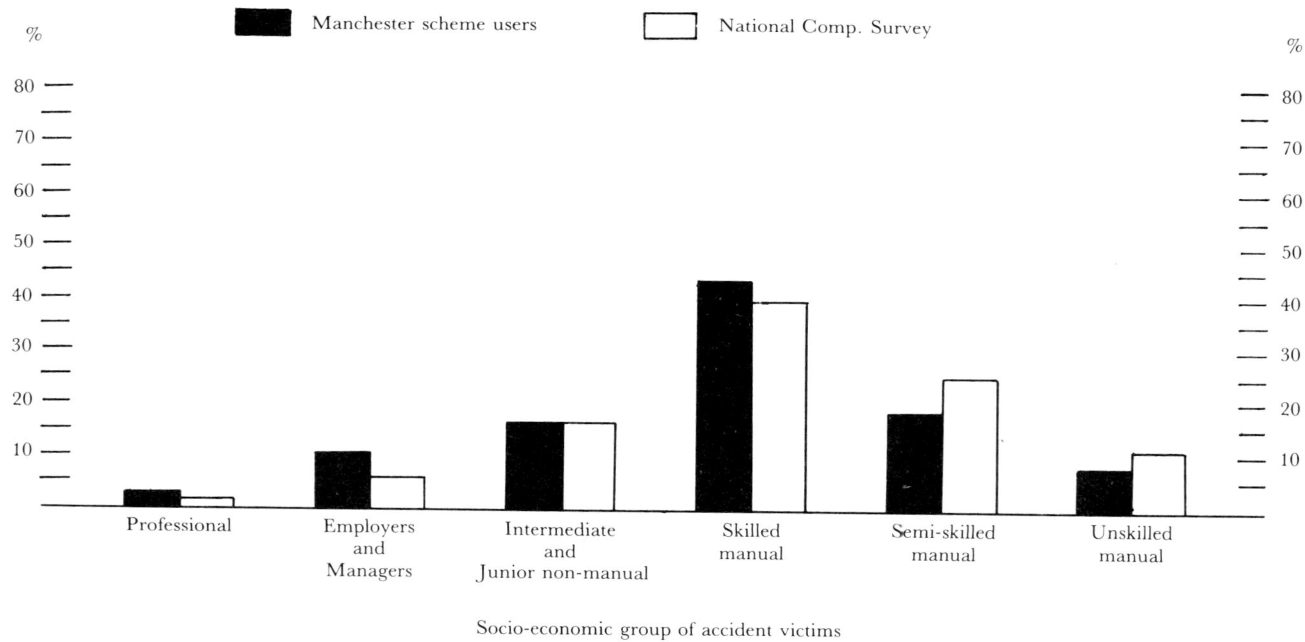

11 per cent of those seeking legal advice had suffered from 'other' types of accidents while 46 per cent were work accident victims and 43 per cent were road accident victims.

Figure 2.5. Comparison of type of accident suffered by Manchester scheme users with type of accident suffered by victims taking legal advice in National Compensation Survey.

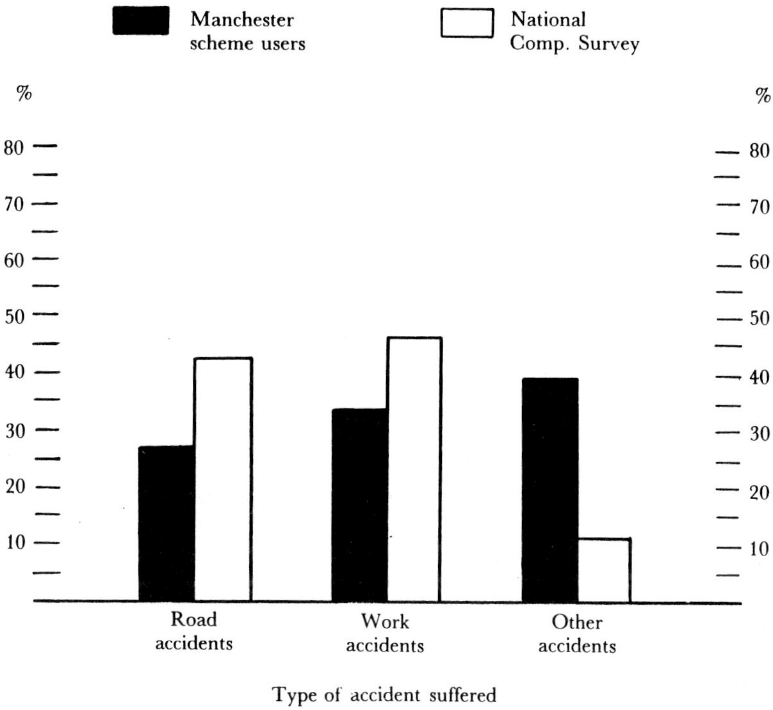

This difference between the findings of the NCS and the analysis of scheme users accounts to some extent for the differences observed above in demographic characteristics of scheme users as compared with data from the NCS, since domestic and leisure accidents disproportionately afflict the elderly, women and children.[2]

In the report of the NCS attention was drawn to the startling differences between the various categories of accident victims in terms of their propensity to seek legal advice. In the case of 'other' accident victims it was suggested that lack of information about claiming compensation was possibly greater than among work or road accident victims and that this fact might provide at least part of the explanation for their failure to seek legal advice:

> "Road and work accident victims suffer injuries in a rather public manner and are attended by policemen, union officials, employers' representatives, etc. In addition, insurance companies are always notified or involved after a motor accident and work accidents are normally noted in accident records. Elsewhere there are no formal or semi-formal procedures for dealing with an accident and the very people who disproportionately suffer those accidents are often isolated from informal networks of information.... If road and work accident victims, with the benefit of these levers into the legal system, succeed in obtaining damages for injuries in only a minority of cases, it is hardly surprising that other accident victims succeed barely at all."[3]

It appears then, on the face of it, that by distributing leaflets which provide both information about making claims for accidents and the offer of some free legal advice, the Manchester scheme has encouraged these victims of 'other' accidents to seek legal advice in considerably greater numbers than would be expected under normal circumstances. Since the number of people suffering accidents in the Greater Manchester area during the period covered by this study is not known, it is impossible to say what proportion of accident victims this represents. It is nevertheless encouraging to observe that the largest proportion of people using the scheme are drawn from the group of accident victims previously identified as having the lowest propensity to seek legal advice following an accident.

3 NATURE AND SEVERITY OF INJURIES

Nearly half of the injuries suffered by users of the scheme were fractures and the remainder were mainly cuts or lacerations, and sprains and strains. Some 12 people (3%) had suffered an amputation of some kind and a similar proportion had sustained head injuries.

It is generally rather difficult to provide any reliable measure of severity of injury, on the basis of survey responses, but we attempted to obtain some indication of this by means of two questions on the postal questionnaire. Respondents were asked first "For how long were you ill after your accident?" and then "Are you still affected by your injuries? If so please say in what way you are affected." The responses to the first of these two questions are summarised in Figure 2.6 below and show that on the basis of information given the majority of scheme users appeared to have been ill for relatively long periods as a result of their accident. This may well be a reflection of the age pattern of users since an elderly person will often take longer to recover from an accident than a younger person with similar injuries, just as older bones being more brittle are more likely to break in a fall than younger bones.

Figure 2.6. *"For how long were you ill after your accident?"*

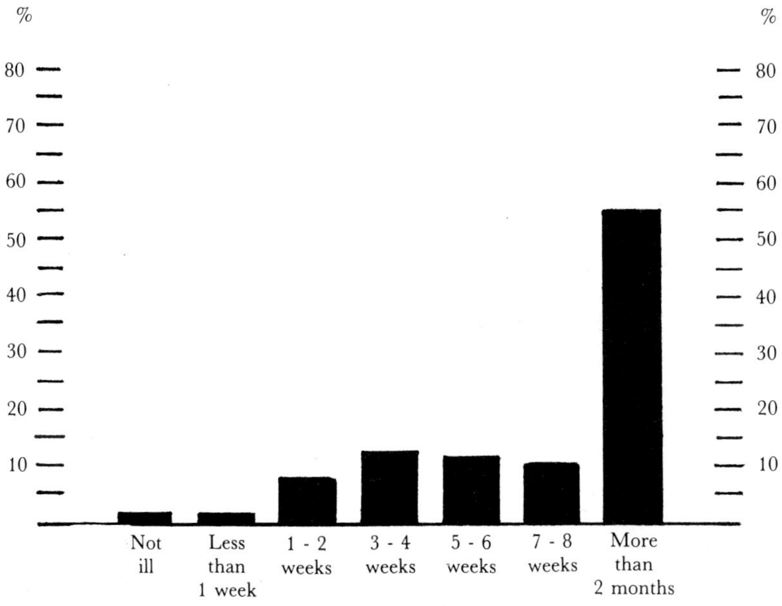

The residual effect of injuries was rather more difficult to assess since this had to be done on the basis of a description given by the respondent. Although the allocation of a response to any particular category was a subjective exercise on the part of the coder, it was at least a consistent allocation since these responses were coded by only one person. The distribution of residual effects is shown in Table 2.1 and shows that just under 10 per cent of scheme users had actually suffered some serious permanent disability. A further 17 per cent (60 people) were still suffering from some serious residual effects of injuries from which they might or might not recover. Thus more than one-quarter of scheme users had suffered from clearly serious injuries and just under a further quarter (22 per cent) were still suffering from moderately serious effects of their injuries.

Table 2.1. *"Are you still affected by your injuries?"*

	No.	%
Permanent serious disability	31	9
Serious residual effects	60	17
Moderate residual effects	76	22
Slight residual effects	75	21
Scar/disfigurement	19	5
Minor amputation	6	2
Nervousness	12	3
Not affected in any way	74	21
	353	100

It was not possible to make any direct comparison between the severity of injuries suffered by scheme users and those suffered by accident victims seeking legal advice in the National Compensation Survey because the relevant questions in the two studies were dissimilar. The information from scheme users, however, indicates that a substantial proportion had suffered from serious injuries and that more than half were still suffering from serious or moderately serious after effects at the time of completing their postal questionnaires.

4 SOURCE OF INFORMATION ABOUT THE SCHEME

Despite the fact that posters and leaflets had been distributed widely to many institutions and agencies it was apparent from information given in questionnaires that Citizens' Advice Bureaux and hospitals were by far the most important sources of information about the scheme. Since it was very difficult for supplies of leaflets to be adequately monitored it is not possible to know whether available posters and leaflets failed to be noticed in other places or whether they were simply rarely displayed and therefore not capable of being noticed.

It was clear on the basis of a spot-check conducted during the course of the survey period that many hospitals had not attempted to replenish supplies of leaflets after they had exhausted their stocks, and that posters advertising the scheme were not often in evidence. It is therefore difficult to estimate the extent to which the importance of CABs as a source of information about the scheme derives from the lack of leaflets and posters elsewhere, and the extent to which coupon returns might be increased if a consistent supply of leaflets could be maintained in hospital casualty and out-patient departments. Those accident victims who had taken the step of enquiring at a CAB in a general way about some sort of redress for their injuries were told about the scheme and handed a leaflet to complete. On the other hand a victim who visited a hospital which was not displaying any literature about the scheme

Figure 2.7. Monthly totals of coupon receipts between March 1979 and December 1980

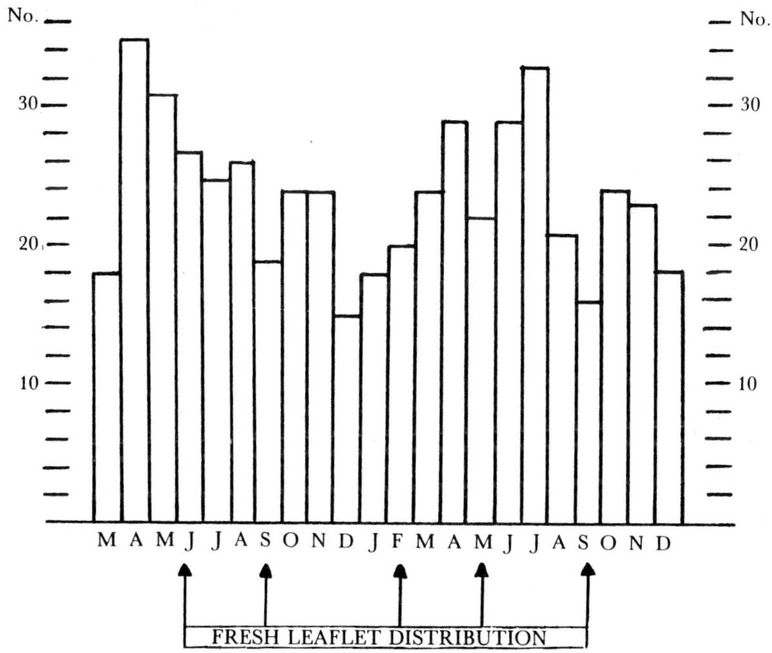

because supplies had run out, would not have had the intended advantage. Figure 2.7 shows that although the number of coupons being received during the study period did not fluctuate greatly from month to month there is clearly an increase in the number being returned following redistributions by the GMLSC. This suggests that a consistent method of maintaining supplies in hospitals and other institutions would improve the level of usage of the scheme.

Despite these difficulties in maintaining supplies, just over one-third of scheme users first found out about the scheme from literature in hospitals (37%), while just under one-half (48%) were informed about the scheme in CABs. The next most important source of information was friends and relations (8%) which indicates that knowledge of the scheme had filtered out into the general community. Some people were actually informed about the scheme by their own solicitors (Table 2.2) and others

Table 2.2. Source of information about scheme

	Road Accidents	Work Accidents	Other Accidents	All Accidents	
	No.	No.	No.	No.	%
Citizens' Advice Bureau	52	54	57	163	48
Hospital[1]	28	49	50	127	37
Friend/relative	6	7	14	27	8
Solicitor	2	1	2	5	1
Library	1	1	2	4	1
Doctor's surgery	1	1	1	3	1
Police	0	0	2	2	1
Other social agency	0	0	2	2	1
Trade Union	2	0	0	2	1
DHSS	1	1	0	2	1
Railway Station	0	1	0	1	*
Town Hall	1	0	0	1	*
Law Centre	0	1	0	1	*
Total No.	94	117	135	340	100

Note
* represents less than 1%

1. Specific hospitals from which leaflets originated are as follows:

	No of cases
Tameside General Hospital	49
Bury General Hospital	10
Withington Hospital	7
North Manchester Hospital	6
Stockport Infirmary	6
Altrincham General	6
Manchester Royal Infirmary	5
Ancoats Hospital	5
Bolton Royal Infirmary	4
Wythenshawe Hospital	4
Park Hospital	4
Salford Royal Hospital	3
Stepping Hill Hospital	2
Crumpsall Hosptial	1
Hope Hosptial	1
Leigh Infirmary	1
Jewish Hospital	1
Blair Hospital	1
Royal Infirmary Wigan	1
Barnsley General Hospital	1
Christies Hospital	1

learnt about the scheme from newspapers or the radio. Posters and leaflets were also found by a few in libraries, DHSS offices, the Town Hall and a railway station.

There was some variation between different types of accident victims in the source of their information about the scheme and this fact is interesting in itself. For example, road accident victims were more likely to have found out about the scheme from a CAB than either work or other accident victims. This suggests that road accident victims either have a more developed claims-consciousness than other types of accident victims or at least have a greater determination to seek some sort of redress. Those people who had suffered domestic or leisure accidents were more likely than road or accident victims to have found out about the scheme through informal sources such as friends and relations.

5 CLAIMS-CONSCIOUSNESS AND PREVIOUS USE OF SOLICITORS

It was clear from responses to the postal questionnaire that many people had at least considered the possibility of trying to obtain compensation before seeing or hearing about the scheme. A little over half (57%) of scheme users said that they had thought about trying to get some compensation before they saw any leaflet or heard about the scheme (Question 2e) and this is borne out to some extent by the high proportion of people who obtained leaflets from CABs and who must have gone there with at least the intention of finding out about the various courses of action which might be open to them. However, information from the National Compensation Survey and from studies of the work done in CABs shows that even amongst the minority of accident victims who actively consider the question of compensation only about half actually go on to obtain legal advice about claiming damages. It is therefore unlikely that without the benefit of the scheme more than a proportion of those actively considering the question of compensation before seeing the leaflets would have sought legal advice at the end of the day.

> "It helped to make my mind up to see a solicitor. The posters and leaflets are displayed so that many people who would not think about claiming are persuaded to try by the posters. I was dithering about going to see a solicitor. The leaflet convinced me that at least I could try for some compensation if a solicitor advised me that I had a claim."

> "At the time of my accident I had not sufficient money to obtain the advice I needed and without the scheme I would probably not have pursued my claim although I thought myself I had a claim." (Work accident: settled for £1,800 plus costs)

Of the 42% of victims who said that they had *not* thought about the possibility of trying to get compensation before seeing a leaflet it is unlikely that more than a very few would have ultimately taken the step of seeking legal advice.

> "People like me who cannot afford to see a solicitor wouldn't have a chance if it wasn't for the free interview ... I wouldn't have even thought about it if it wasn't for the leaflet the nurse had given me at the hospital."

Again evidence from research indicates that in the majority of successful claims for damages, advice about claiming is sought very soon after the accident and that the longer an individual delays after the occurrence of the accident before seeking legal advice, the less chance there is that a claim will be successful.''[4]

Despite the fact that a large number of scheme users had not considered the question of compensation *before* finding a leaflet the majority of users, when they sent in their coupon, had some idea against whom they might make a claim. Only 16 people said that they didn't know against whom to claim. The reasons given for thinking that they might be able to make a claim against the specified person or body were most often related to feelings that the person had been negligent, in some way at fault, or somehow responsible for the accident which had occurred. Others simply referred to the injury or their suffering; to the financial loss which they had suffered or to the idea that the person was insured against such contingencies.

The identity of the people against whom coupon users thought they might be able to claim when they returned their coupons is

Table 2.3. *''When you sent in your coupon WHO did you think you might be able to claim compensation from?''*

	No.	%
Employer	115	33
Local Council	79	23
Other driver	71	20
Public transport	19	5
Shop owner	14	4
Owner recreational facilities	8	2
Driver's employer	5	1
Area health authority	5	1
CICB/MIB	4	1
Manufacturer	3	1
Neighbour	2	1
Landlord	2	1
Utility	1	*
Builder	1	*
Worker's employer	1	*
Other person	4	1
Didn't know	16	5
	350	100

Note
* represents less than 1%

summarised in Table 2.3 and their reasons for thinking that they might be able to claim are summarised in Table 2.4.

Table 2.4. *"Why did you think that you might be able to claim compensation from them?"*

	No.	%
Negligence	127	39
Responsibility	57	17
Fault	52	16
Injury/suffering	25	8
Advised by other	23	7
Loss suffered	16	5
Because defendant insured	11	3
Injury and responsibility	10	3
Don't know	5	1
	326	100

The people using the scheme had, on the whole, little experience of using solicitors' services in the past. Nearly two-thirds of scheme users had never consulted a solicitor before about any matter (62%) and this lack of experience clearly accounts in part for the extreme nervousness expressed by many in relation to solicitors and legal matters. Whether or not a scheme user had previously consulted a solicitor did not seem to influence the way in which he came to find out about the scheme. So, for example, those who had had some experience of legal services were not more likely to have found out about the scheme through a CAB than those who had no experience of legal matters.

> "I must say not having been for an interview before I was struck by the helpfulness of the solicitor. My workmates, family and friends are totally ignorant of aspects of the law. I now know that legal aid or legality is open to all, not just the rich but the lowly as well."

NOTES

1 See Appendix 1 for a discussion of response to the postal questionnaire.

2 The findings of the National Compensation Survey indicate that the rates for different types of accident resulting in serious injury are as follows:

Rates per 1000

	Road Accidents	Work Accidents	Other Accidents	Total
Sex				
Male	3.0	6.1	30.5	39.6
Female	1.3	1.0	38.1	40.4
Age				
0-15	1.1	0.0	17.9	19.0
16-24	1.3	1.6	23.6	26.5
25-34	2.6	8.5	24.6	37.5
35-54	2.6	7.3	27.6	37.5
55-64	4.1	3.0	47.9	54.9
65 +	1.8	0.2	84.5	86.5

Chapter 1. *Compensation and Support,* op. cit.

3 H. G. Genn, ''Who Claims Compensation?'' Ch. 2 in D. Harris et al, *Compensation and Support for Illness and Injury, op. cit.*

4 D. Harris, ''Claims for Damages'', Ch. 3 in D. Harris et al, *Compensation and Support, op.cit.*

3

The Outcome of Free Interviews

It was suggested earlier that one important criterion of the success of the accident leaflet scheme would be whether it was actually tapping a reservoir of unmet need for legal services. Apart from the expectations of accident victims using the scheme, from the viewpoint of solicitors the effort involved in encouraging accident victims to seek legal advice about claiming damages might only be considered worthwhile if the final result indicated that such people actually had good causes of action.

It has not been uncommon in the past for practising lawyers to assume that those people who fail to seek legal advice following an accident do so because they do not have viable claims for damages. This contention assumes that reluctance to seek legal advice stems from a reasonable assessment by the injured victim of his chances of succeeding with a claim. If this were the case it would suggest a degree of legal sophistication and claims-consciousness which is not borne out by any of the research which has been carried out into this subject. As it has been seen, this research indicates that factors like fear of legal costs, ignorance of the Legal Aid scheme, and a general failure to consider the question of compensation after an accident are much more likely to prevent people from obtaining legal advice than any calm analysis in legal terms of the strengths and weaknesses of their claim. If this were true, then a scheme designed to break down some of the barriers to claiming and to encourage accident victims to consult solicitors would in theory produce at least as many injured victims with good causes of action as those without.

Bearing these issues in mind the proportion of free interviews provided by solicitors which resulted in a claim being taken up are discussed in this chapter; and following that, the proportion of claims taken up that resulted in a successful settlement between the parties is analysed.

1 ADVICE GIVEN AT FREE INTERVIEW

(a) *Claims taken up*

All respondents to the postal questionnaire were asked what their solicitor had advised them to do on the basis of the initial free interview (Q3a. "When you went to see the solicitor what did he advise you to do and what reasons did he give you for his advice?"). Information obtained in the questionnaires indicated that just over *three-quarters* (76%) of all accident victims were advised at the outset that they had a cause of action and that the solicitor was willing to take on the case (Table 3.1). In a further four per cent of cases some action to recover damages was subsequently taken. In total then, *80 per cent of the free interviews granted resulted in some action being taken* by solicitors to obtain compensation. This figure appears surprisingly high given that all people returning a coupon from a leaflet were granted a free interview with no intermediate screening of any kind. The apparently low level of dubious claims suggests that the scheme is neither being abused nor misused, something to which solicitors particularly drew attention, as will be seen in Chapter 5.

Table 3.1. Advice given at free interview

	Road accidents	Work accidents	Other accidents	All accidents	
	%	%	%	%	No.
Advised to make a claim	89	77	77	80	269
Advised NOT to claim	10	19	18	16	58
Other action advised[1]	1	4	5	3	11
Total %	100	100	100	100	
Total No.	95	120	138		353

Note
1. "other action advised" comprises such things as being advised to accept an offer already made (3 cases); seeking advice from a Union, etc.

The proportion of clients being advised to make a claim varied somewhat according to the type of accident suffered. Road accident victims were the group most likley to be advised to proceed with a claim, followed by work and 'other' accident victims. The proportions were 89%, 77% and 77% respectively (Table 3.1). The figure for victims of accidents other than on the road or at work is especially interesting. These victims of domestic and leisure accidents in normal circumstances rarely even consider the possibility of claiming compensation and are conventionally thought as a group to have only a meagre chance of successfully identifying and suing a negligent defendant.

In the analysis of the advice given at the free interview in relation to other characteristics of the accident victims, no difference overall between men and women was found in the extent to which their claims were taken up (see Table 3.2 below). Although women suffering accidents at work were proportionately more likely than other groups to be advised not to proceed with a claim, this was counterbalanced in general by the fact that women who had had road accidents were the group which most often had claims taken up by solicitors (Table 3.2). As far as the age of the accident victim was concerned, although there were differences in the rate at which claims were taken up between different age groups there was no consistent pattern. The elderly were just as likely as younger people to be advised to proceed with a claim despite the fact that they have previously been found to be

Table 3.2. Outcome of free interview in relation to sex of scheme user and type of accident suffered

	Males				Females			
	Road	Work	Other	All	Road	Work	Other	All
	%	%	%	%	%	%	%	%
No claim made	14	17	22	16	5	26	18	17
Claim made	86	83	78	84	95	74	82	83
Total %	100	100	100	100	100	100	100	100
Total No.	57	78	23	158	37	38	109	184

especially unlikely as a group to seek legal advice (see earlier Chapter 2). Indeed the take-up rate for the 70 plus age group was the same as that for the age group 30 to 39.

(b) *Claims not taken up*

In only 58 cases (16 per cent of all free interviews) did solicitors advise at the outset that no action should be taken to recover compensation. The reasons given on the postal questionnaire (where known) for this are as follows:

Difficult to prove negligence	11 cases
No negligence by third party	9 cases
Victim's own fault	7 cases
Claim out of time	6 cases
Not worth taking action	6 cases
Not enough evidence	5 cases
Paving stone not bad enough	3 cases
Border-line claim	2 cases
"Hopeless case"	1 case

Since these 'reasons' are based on respondents' memory of what was said at the interview and were often presented on the questionnaire in the vernacular, it is difficult to assess the extent to which the above categories are an accurate representation of what actually passed between solicitors and their clients. They are, however, consistent with the findings of the National Compensation Survey.

2 RESULTS OF ACTION TAKEN

All respondents to the postal questionnaire who stated that the solicitor had taken some action to recover compensation for them were asked: "What is the position of the claim now?" Of the 284 cases in which action was taken just over one-quarter (26%) had been settled at the time respondents completed the questionnaire and just over a further two-fifths (41%) of respondents stated that the claim was still unsettled. Another fifth (21%) said that they did not know what the position of the claim was at that time. In 12 per cent of cases claims had been abandoned at the time the questionnaire was completed.

On the basis of this information then nearly two-thirds of claims taken up were still apparently outstanding at the time completed postal questionnaires were returned. It was therefore decided to seek information directly from solicitors as to their assessment of the chances of the outstanding claims being successfully settled, and further, for information as to the actual status of claims where the claimant himself had not known the position.

From the replies received from solicitors it was found that in the period intervening between receipt of postal questionnaires from clients and receipt of questionnaires from solicitors a further 44 cases had been settled, 13 had been abandoned and 90 were still being negotiated. Replies from solicitors were not received for 28 of the outstanding claims.

The information received about the position of claims from both claimants and solicitors is combined and summarised in Table 3.3 which shows a relatively high level of success. *In 83 per cent of claims taken up by solicitors a settlement had either been reached or was still being negotiated* and only 47 claims (16 per cent) had been abandoned.

Table 3.3. Result of action taken by solicitors

	Road Accidents	Work Accidents	Other Accidents	All Accidents	
	%	%	%	%	No.
Claim settled	49	40	38	42	119
Negotiations continuing	42	45	38	41	118
Claim abandoned	9	15	23	16	47
Total %	100	100	100	100	
Total No.	84	93	107		284

(a) *Settled claims*

From Table 3.3 it can be seen that road accident victims had the highest level of success in settling their claims followed by work and then 'other' accident victims. Just under half of all claims for road accidents had been settled by the end of the study period with some 42 per cent still outstanding and under negotiation. Work accident claims had been settled in 40 per cent of cases with a further 45 per cent of claims still under negotiation; and 'other' accident claims had a slightly lower success rate with 38 per cent being settled by the end of the study and with a further 38 per cent still being negotiated.

(b) *Amounts of settlements*

Both clients and solicitors were asked to say on the questionnaire what amount had been obtained from the other side in all cases where claims had been settled. In all but six of the known settlements this information was provided. Table 3.4 shows the distribution of settlements which ranged from £50 to £30,000. These figures are *exclusive* of costs. The total amount of damages recovered by respondents by the end of the study period was £136,742 and the average amount obtained was £1,210 although this figure is somewhat inflated by the one large award of £30,000. The median amount obtained was £600 and this is a better reflection of the true average. Just under one-third of all settlements were for more than £1,000.

Road accident victims in general obtained the highest level of settlements with an average of £1,853, while the average for work accidents was £1,227 and 'other' accident victims obtained an average settlement of £647. The average for road accidents is inflated by the award for £30,000 and the average for 'other' accidents reflects the fact that in many cases damages would have represented compensation only for non-pecuniary loss. All but 9 of the settled claims of 'other' accident victims were by women, the majority of whom were not in paid employment.

It is difficult to compare the amounts of settlements with the findings of the National Compensation Survey because of the influence of inflation on amounts. In that survey the average amount of damages obtained was £1,135 with a median of £500. However, most of those settlements were obtained between 1973 and 1977 so the figures are not really amenable to comparison.

(c) *Unsettled claims*

As a result of the length of time which often elapses between the

Table 3.4. Amounts of known settlements (exclusive of costs)

	No.	%	Cum. %
£1-99	2	2	2
£100 +	9	8	10
£200 +	8	7	17
£300 +	10	9	26
£400 +	12	11	37
£500 +	12	11	48
£600 +	12	11	59
£700 +	4	3	62
£800 +	5	4	66
£900 +	2	2	68
£1000 +	26	23	91
£2000 +	6	5	96
£3000 +	1	1	97
£4000 +	0		
£5000 +	4	3	100
	113	100	

Notes

Range of settlements = £50-£30,000
Total amount obtained = £136,742.00
Average amount obtained = £1,210.00
Median amount obtained = £600.00

initiation of a claim for damages and the ultimate settlement of that claim, it was to be expected that a high proportion of claims taken up would not have reached a conclusion by the time the study period ended. It was nevertheless felt that some sort of assessment from solicitors as to the chances of a successful settlement being reached in these claims, would help to provide a more complete picture. In all claims still apparently outstanding at the time postal questionnaires were received back from scheme users, solicitors were sent a very brief slip requesting information about the status of the claim. Where the solicitor indicated that a claim was still unsettled he was asked: "In your opinion what are the plaintiff's chances of success in this case?" and required to choose from the following categories:

0-25% / 26-50% / 51-75% / More than 75%

Information was received back from solicitors for all but 32 of the 118 unsettled claims and their replies are summarised in Table 3.5 below.

Table 3.5 Solicitors' assessment of chances of success in unsettled claims

	Number of cases
0-25%	6
26-50%	13
51-75%	24
More than 75%	43
Unknown	32
Total No.	118

Of the 43 cases which were estimated by solicitors to have more than a 75% chance of success, six plaintiffs had already rejected offers made by the defendant's insurers.

(d) *Abandoned claims*

Of the 47 claims which were apparently abandoned after some action to recover damages was taken by a solicitor, the reasons for abandonment were obtained in 35 cases. In 22 of these cases the reason was supplied by the scheme user on the postal questionnaire and in 13 cases the reason was given by the solicitor on a questionnaire requesting information about current status of outstanding claims. Since the two sets of reasons are not compatible they are presented separately below:

Reasons for abandoning claims given by scheme users

Insurance Company denied liability	7 cases
Couldn't get Legal Aid	6 cases
Afraid of cost of proceeding	3 cases
Solicitor incompetent	2 cases
Not enough evidence	2 cases
Afraid of cost of going to court	1 case
Claim made too late	1 case

Reasons for abandoned claims given by solicitors

Negligence couldn't be established	5 cases
No real cause of action	2 cases
No instructions to proceed	2 cases
Witnesses unfavourable	1 case
Liability denied	1 case
Client couldn't provide enough information	1 case
Accident was client's own fault	1 case

These abandoned cases, perhaps predictably, were the source of the greatest dissatisfaction expressed both with solicitors and with the scheme in general. Those clients who received a free interview and were told at the outset that it was probably not worth pursuing a claim or that they had no cause of action in law, tended to accept the advice on the whole without complaint or disagreement.

Those clients who were advised to proceed with a claim which subsequently proved fruitless, or where they felt that to carry on might be too great a gamble, were often bitter about their experience. There was evidence of misunderstanding on the part of scheme users as to the prospects of their claim and also evidence that solicitors did not always make clear what the cost of taking action might be in the event of failure of negotations:

> "The scheme could be a good thing provided solicitors do not raise false hopes as my experience proved. I was given the impression in the first place that I had a good chance of settlement, but once my employers showed they intended to fight my claim the solicitor discouraged me from going on, when I had paid out almost £100 in physiotherapy bills." [The accident victim had opted for private treatment rather than waiting a long time for NHS treatment, in the expectation that the costs would have been covered by damages]

> "Theoretically it would seem a good idea and in the course of my hospital work I have since recommended it to patients on occasion. Much depends on the individual solicitor to whom one is referred. As far as I personally am concerned however, it led to unnecessary expense. The interview time was changed several times at short notice and was eventually crowded in very

early one morning, in great haste. Once the Council repudiated liability ... the solicitor decided that one would need to press the matter very hard, incur considerable costs, and be unlikely to cover them.... I paid off the solicitor being both unwilling and unable to incur any further expense and have since pursued the matter myself."

> "In small claims I think the solicitors should state definitely regarding cost of letters. In my case it cost £23.00 ... after contractor denied liability I heard nothing till I received a bill for the amount stated."

The difficulties of obtaining Legal Aid were the cause for strong comment, as was the problem of meeting the required contribution in the case of limited Legal Aid. This is discussed again in Chapter 4.

> "I think that it is a good thing, but it still cost me quite a sum of money for letters sent, appointments made etc., in solicitors' fees, and then having to drop the claim in the end because I couldn't get Legal Aid and couldn't afford to take the matter to Court."

> "I think the Legal Aid levels need urgent review, as costs deter people proceeding especially against large organizations. It didn't help me personally."

3 IDENTITY OF DEFENDANTS

Those people who took some action to recover compensation were asked against whom their claim had been made. Not all respondents to the postal questionnaire were sure who the defendant was, but the information given on questionnaires is summarised in Table 3.6.

Table 3.6 Identity of Defendants

Defendant	No. of cases	%
Employer	82	33
Other driver	51	21
Local Council	51	21
Public Transport	15	6
Shop Owner	9	4
Driver's Employer	9	4
CICB/MIB	9	4
Utility	5	2
Driver of victim's car	5	2
Owner of recreational facilities	5	2
Landlord	1	*
Manufacturer	1	*
Area Health Authority	1	*
School	1	*
Neighbour	1	*
Other	2	1
	248	100%

Note: * represents less than 1%

4

Scheme users' views

The analysis of personal characteristics of scheme users together with the analysis of outcome of claims suggests that the scheme *is* stimulating successful claims from accident victims who might normally be expected to be unlikely to seek legal advice. This, it is hoped, is an objective assessment of the impact of the scheme; but what of the perceptions of users of the scheme? Do they *feel* that the scheme has been of assistance to them and to what extent are they satisfied with the way in which it operates? These perceptions are valuable not only as an alternative way of looking at the success of the scheme, but also as an indication of the aspects of the scheme which are most important to those who use it and as a guide to areas for improvement.

1 SATISFACTION WITH SOLICITORS

The vast majority of scheme users expressed satisfaction both with the advice and service they received from their solicitors, almost irrespective of the content of the advice. To an extent, this is not particularly surprising since it is very difficult for most clients to assess the advice they are given. It is however encouraging to find that many accident victims had experienced kindness and attention from their solicitors in excess of their expectations:

> "The advice and encouragement I have received from my solicitor under the scheme has been all and more than I could have wished for ... I did not think for one moment that I would receive the attention I have bearing in mind that the scheme is free"

> "It is the first time I have seen a solicitor and he made me feel quite at ease and was very helpful"

"I thought my solicitor could not have been more helpful. As I am deaf my sister came with me and he asked her to make sure that I understood everything he had explained before the interview ended"

"I cannot speak highly enough of the advice we were given or the way we were treated"

A minority of respondents said that they had been satisfied initially with the advice they had received but later changed their opinion as a result of things that occurred during the course of the claim. For example, many people were bitterly unhappy about the length of time which the claim was taking to be settled and, perhaps unfairly, assumed that their solicitor was responsible for the inordinate delay. Although delay is often unavoidable in personal injury actions it is clear that clients were in the main unprepared for this and lack of communication from their solicitor may have exacerbated the problem:

"The free interview scheme is very good ... I have been disappointed that my claim has not been settled. I have lost working time going to the solicitor's office and for medical examinations. I do not know who is at fault but feel that two years and two months is a long time."

"I have been very disappointed with the solicitor's performance ... I don't think we have gone very far with the case considering it is nearly *TWO* years since I first made my claim." (Work accident involving amputation)

"The scheme has put my mind at ease. I would not know how to start or even come up with a figure if I had not had the help of a solicitor . . . I am only surprised that I have not been made an offer after nearly twelve months and cannot understand why it should take so long."

The difficulty about delays was understood more clearly by some respondents and one road accident victim succinctly expressed his attitude to the problem:

> "It is an excellent scheme in principle, but personally I feel it would take more than a solicitor to fight their way past Insurance Companies' continual prevarication. Probably divine intervention would be the best bet."

About 50 people were clearly dissatisfied with the advice they received and this often coloured their view of the scheme in general. Complaints tended to be based on a lack of confidence in the advice they were given or on a perceived lack of interest or offhand manner on the part of the solicitor. Although clients may sometimes misconstrue advice or be oversensitive to a busy solicitor, in some cases there was apparently good reason for concern. For example:

> "I think the free interview is alright for anybody who hasn't got any money. The solicitor gives the impression that you are not paying him and he gives the impression that he wants to get rid of your case as soon as possible and wants you to accept any offers given by the guilty party. Also he is hard to contact and always takes days to answer my inquiries."

In particular there were several cases where the solicitor had advised the client not to proceed and the client subsequently succeeded in reaching a settlement by negotiating personally with the defendant. An example was a 62 year old woman who had suffered a work accident while employed as a nursing assistant. She had found an accident leaflet in the outpatients department of a hospital she was attending and anticipated a claim against the Area Health Authority.

> "The solicitor told me that it was impossible to get damages for loss of earnings from the Area Health Authority. In his experience they never paid any and I may as well go and bang my head against a wall ... I was rather upset but after a few weeks I decided to fight the case myself. I have obtained myself £2,750 and £650 a year for life ... In my opinion the solicitor I saw was not in the least interested ... he was most unhelpful ... I am concerned that someone else in the position I was in may be too disheartened to follow it up as I did."

Another scheme user, a road accident victim, who finally settled his claim through a different firm of solicitors had some harsh criticism for the solicitor originally assigned to the case:

> "The solicitor was brash, arrogant, unhelpful, appeared bored with his work and was generally useless. I was not satisfied with his attitude"

Although such fiercely negative attitudes represented only a small minority they nevertheless suggest that there is room for improvement in the quality of service being offered by some firms.

2 VALUE OF THE SCHEME

It was suggested in the introductory chapter that there are three important hurdles which accident victims must overcome before they are likely to seek legal advice about making a claim for compensation, and that the accident leaflet scheme might have the following benefits: (i) increasing knowledge about the possibility of claiming amongst accident victims; (ii) reducing or eliminating fears of legal costs; and (iii) providing easy access to solicitors for people with little or no experience of using legal services. The often lengthy comments given on the postal questionnaires by users of the scheme provide a rich source of documentation of the extent to which these factors restrain accident victims from seeking legal advice. In addition, the comments spotlight the strain and trauma which frequently flow from even relatively minor accidents and the extent to which sympathetic and constructive legal advice may help to relieve this burden. There is clearly room for many solicitors to develop a 'bedside manner'.

Nearly three-quarters of the views expressed about the scheme were unreservedly positive. Even those people who had been advised not to proceed with a claim or who had abandoned a claim after taking some action were often enthusiastic about the idea of the scheme:

> "Obviously I think it a worthwhile scheme and for many it may prove profitable as they may through it get some compensation they would not otherwise have thought themselves entitled to. It

has not helped me personally but I am only one in thousands. Keep up the good work.''

''I think it is a very good scheme for people like me who can't afford solicitors' fees. Unfortunately I wasn't helped, but I don't think that has any bearing on how I feel.''

Not surprisingly, those people who had already settled their claims by the time they completed the postal questionnaire were often quite exuberant about the scheme:

''I think the scheme about the free interview is brilliant because I had no person or institution to turn to. Non union etc.etc., so what could I do?'' (Work accident settled)

''I think it is absolutely fantastic that there is such a scheme, otherwise I should not have got anywhere without it. (I) would not have gone otherwise as I could not have afforded the money owing to being only on invalidity pension for the last 4 years.'' (Road accident settled)

Among those scheme users who felt that the scheme had been helpful to them, remarks most often related to their prior fears of legal costs. More than half of the respondents commenting said that they had been afraid of legal costs or that they would not have been able to afford to see a solicitor. In addition, however, to this preoccupation with costs there was also clear expression of uncertainty about legal rights and how to go about finding and instructing a solicitor.

(a) *Improving knowledge about claiming*

In Chapter 2 it was seen that some 42 per cent of all scheme users stated that they had *not* thought about trying to get some compensation before seeing or hearing of the leaflets. This finding was confirmed in comments describing how the scheme had helped the accident victims personally. For example, a motor cyclist involved in an accident with a car had found a leaflet in the Accident Department of the hospital to which he was taken, obtained an interview and settled his claim for £1,200. He said:

"I thought (the scheme) was very good. Everything was explained in full. If I had not seen the poster I would not have known about it. So I would have not made a claim!"

A 66 year old woman who broke her wrist in a work accident found a leaflet in a hospital and obtained just under £200 from her employers:

"I think it is very good and I would not have got anything if I had not seen the leaflet at the hospital"

A work accident victim who settled his claim for £450 had visited the CAB and been told about the scheme. He said:

"I think the scheme is very worthwhile because a person can find out his rights from qualified people instead of listening to barrack room lawyers and other misinformed sources. In my own case I did not know such a scheme existed until I went to the CAB. Also I did not know whether or not I had a case and against who, until I saw the solicitor."

Among those people who had been vaguely considering the idea of trying to obtain compensation or those who felt some sort of redress ought to be available, the leaflets often provided a necessary 'push' in the right direction:

"I thought I might be eligible for compensation but I didn't know where to start ... I probably wouldn't have made a claim if it hadn't been for the scheme as I didn't know what to do and I wouldn't have gone to a solicitor privately as I didn't know if it was worthwhile claiming or even if I had grounds for a claim."

"I think the scheme is extremely helpful and encourages people like myself to take that important first step towards seeking legal advice which we are often reluctant to do for various reasons."

The advantages of an easily accessible source of information about the possibility of claiming compensation were also, evidently, not confined to the period immediately following an accident. There were a number of claimants who came across leaflets some time after their accident had occurred. In some cases it was so long after the event that solicitors advised that the claim was actually barred by the Limitation Act, but for others the claim was still viable:

> "It was rather by chance that I spotted the leaflet and it was later on in my accident. It must have been three months later that I saw and filled out the leaflet."

In one particularly tragic case a scheme user had visited a solicitor two years previously but had abandoned her claim on her husband's behalf when she failed to obtain Legal Aid because she felt she could not afford to gamble with what money she had. Although her husband had been irreversibly brain damaged in a road accident she had taken no further action after her initial abortive attempt at claiming compensation. She found an accident leaflet in a doctor's surgery in 1980 and said:

> "For me personally it made me think again about seeing a solicitor."

She obtained a free interview and although was refused Legal Aid again the solicitor proceeded with the claim and obtained a settlement of £30,000 in respect of her husband's injuries. She said:

> "I wanted to try to get compensation for my husband, as I had been told by his doctor that he would never be able to come home and always have to stay in hospital. He is now 30 years old."

(b) *Reducing fears of legal costs*

Fear of the expense involved in seeking legal advice was so pervasive amongst the people using the scheme that it was difficult to select quotations. The extent to which the accident victims were ignorant of the Legal Aid and Legal Advice schemes is disconcerting, but goes a long way towards providing an explanation for their fears:

> "The scheme is excellent as it helps people find out about their rights. People who would be afraid to pursue a claim because of the cost involved have now the opportunity to carry on. The law applies to rich and poor alike and lack of funds is now no excuse. I would not have gone to see a solicitor. I would have been afraid to be left with no compensation plus all the costs to find with no resources"

> "I think the scheme is excellent. I had considered taking legal advice but nerves and thoughts of huge solicitors' fees put me off. The offer of a free interview with reputable solicitors is something more people should be made aware of and therefore used."

> "I think the scheme is very helpful in that I learned of things such as Legal Aid, that I was not previously aware of."

> "Many people probably hesitate to take legal advice because of the worry of legal fees. The free interview scheme benefits these people especially if they are in financial difficulties because of an accident or dispute of some nature. It is reassuring to know that it is available."

> "I think it is an excellent idea because at the time I would not have considered going to a solicitor because of the cost and I did not have any money with having to pay for my motorcycle. I think a lot of people would be in this situation and that the scheme should be more widely publicised."

Even in cases where accident victims had been advised informally that they ought to try and claim some compensation, it was their apprehension about further strain on their financial resources that prevented them from taking any action:

> "Everyone had advised me to claim compensation but I did not know how to go about it. At the time I could not work due to my back injury and so finances were low. I felt that going to a solicitor for his advice would be very expensive initially ... so the free interview scheme was obviously a help to me as I could not have afforded a solicitor. The scheme must help hundreds

of people in a similar situation and I think it should be more widely publicised."

"My son picked up (the leaflet) at the hospital thinking it might be useful to me. I wasn't thinking of compensation at that time, just advice from a solicitor regarding my rights as the innocent party. The solicitor interviewed me at my home as I was incapacitated with my leg in a plaster cast. The interview took place without the anxiety I might have felt if I had had to pay - at that time I was terribly worried about my not working and how I was going to cope financially. Not knowing how I stood as far as making a claim for compensation, I think I may have hesitated about going to a solicitor for advice. As things are, I have been advised regarding Legal Aid, and I feel confident about the future now."

There was evidence, however, that despite the advantages of the free interview in providing information about Legal Aid to those with limited resources, severe difficulties had been experienced by some of those who had applied for Legal Aid:

"It has helped me to fight for my wages which I lost but I don't think I could go through it again. What stopped me from fighting on was the payments to the Law Society. I could not just keep up with the payments. It's O.K. putting two wages together as they do but things don't work out like that at home and having three children. In my mind I go to work to help support my family and I never get the time to save. I have found all this a great strain so I went to my solicitor and told him to settle my claim."

"My solicitor applied for legal aid on my behalf. This was refused, why I do not know because as a widow I am dependent on my small savings and live in dread that I may not have enough to pay my solicitor should I fail. I found it extremely nerve-wracking having to get together all the documents required by the Law Society. I was still turned down, still left with my injuries and still unable to understand why so many get help and I was turned down."

In the vast majority of cases, however, the offer of some free legal advice came as a welcome source of relief and represented an opportunity for accident victims to recoup some or all of their losses.

> "I feel the scheme is very good because when people come to make a claim more often than not they have been off work for some time and are not well off. The thought of a solicitor's bill would frighten most off, and a lot of people would be frightened to make a claim. Your scheme helps people in this position and the advice they receive enables them to know exactly how they stand without getting into debt. For that reason I feel this scheme is very good for the working class.

(c) *Improving accessibility of solicitors*

It was seen in Chapter 2 that nearly two-thirds of the accident victims making use of the free interview scheme had never previously consulted a solicitor on any matter. The effect of this lack of experience was evident in many of the comments made both in relation to the perceived difficulty of *finding* a solicitor to instruct and apprehension as to what might occur when the interview took place. There is obviously considerable confusion as to how a solicitor should be found or selected and this general confusion tends to increase at a time when people may be distressed and not thinking very clearly.

> "The scheme helped me immensely. As being in a state of shock at the time and did not know quite what to do, I telephoned the Citizens' Advice Bureau, who were most kind and helpful and told me of the scheme, so they sent me the form to fill in, upon which I was then advised to see the solicitor whom you recommended"

> "This is an excellent scheme particularly for someone like myself who had no experience of solicitors and am not a member of a union. I expected to be recommended to a solicitor suitable for my case (and was not disappointed) as against asking around on my own and possibly selecting one who was not suitable."

"It gives you the first contact with the solicitor. It saves you the worry of having to look around and making an appointment with a solicitor. Because if it's the first time you have been in contact with a solicitor it can be quite off-putting not knowing what to expect."

"I think the scheme is very good especially for people like myself who have no idea how to go about anything like this.'

"It put my mind at rest as to what to do about going about a claim. I don't think I would have gone to see a solicitor if not for picking up the leaflet."

In addition to the theoretical difficulties perceived by accident victims in finding a solicitor to deal with their claim for compensation, there are also practical problems which prevent contact being made; viz. the *physical* difficulty that an injured person may have in actually visiting a solicitor. Those who are immobilised or whose mobility is seriously limited for a long time after the accident may not be aware that solicitors will often be prepared to interview a client at his home or in hospital. People with no experience of solicitors might be hesitant about requesting a home visit even if the possibility had occurred to them. For those using the scheme, filling out the coupon on an accident leaflet required no special physical effort and when contact was made subsequently by the solicitor assigned to the client, these problems were often overcome. For example a 75 year old woman had been unable to get out for some time after her accident. While waiting for an ambulance to take her home after a hospital visit for physiotherapy she saw a poster advertising the scheme on the wall and asked for a leaflet:

"I had the leaflet for weeks before I sent the coupon in. I felt too ill to bother. My friends and neighbours told me I was mad ... The solicitor has been very helpful. He has visited me at my home because I cannot get to him. When I explained it was going to be difficult to get to his office he said he would come to see me which I appreciated very much."

In general, then, the views of the scheme expressed by those who had made use of it were extremely encouraging. Such criticism as existed tended to relate to an unhappy experience with the particular solicitor assigned to the client, rather than to any doubts about the value of the scheme itself. Many people felt that the scheme had not been publicised widely enough; for example, a man who fell down an uncovered man-hole and found a leaflet in the casualty department of a hospital:

> "I think the scheme is an excellent idea and should receive better publicity so that everyone is aware of it. If the scheme had not been in existence I would probably not have pursued my case."

The scheme appears to be very much appreciated by people who have little knowledge about their rights, and scant experience of using legal services.

> "I think possibly the most important thing about any scheme like this free advice is that it takes a tremendous weight off one's mind especially in the early stages. Very often people just don't know what to do, but just about everyone wants to tell you. Professional help and advice is a genuine comfort."

5

Solicitors' views

Although an impression of solicitors' experiences in operating the free interview scheme was felt to be an important aspect of the evaluation, it was nevertheless rather difficult to obtain representative views from solicitors. First, many of the solicitors involved in the scheme had only interviewed two or three clients by the end of the study period and were therefore not in a position to make generalisations. Secondly, most solicitors did not take the opportunity offered in questionnaires to comment on their experience of the scheme. This chapter is therefore based on views obtained from a dozen firms who wrote comments on questionnaires, and on information obtained from telephone interviews with some of those firms which had dealt with a large number of clients through the scheme.

1 THE CLIENTS

In general, comments obtained from solicitors were favourable in relation to the clients to whom free interviews had been granted and also tended to confirm some of the assumptions made earlier about why accident victims hesitate to seek legal advice. Solicitors found that on the whole clients using the scheme *did* have good causes of action and that the potential claims were not more dubious or of a lower value than those personal injury cases which come to them through normal channels. They did not feel that the scheme was being abused and said they thought the clients seen would probably *not* have obtained legal advice had it not been for the existence of the scheme:

> "This is a substantial claim - possibly worth in excess of £15,000; almost inevitably one can say that was it not for the Accident Leaflet Scheme this particular plaintiff would probably not even have considered consulting a Solicitor."

Many solicitors were aware of the apprehension felt by accident victims about consulting a solicitor and a number commented particularly on the fact that elderly people seen under the scheme had previously been frightened of going to a solicitor:

> "A visit to a solicitor is something very unusual ... people say afterwards, 'well I didn't think it was going to be like this!' "

> "This is a particularly worthwhile scheme in that if the claim is successful then there will invariably be a benefit - however great or small - for the client at the end of the day. It appears that many people simply do not know or even think of the possibility that there may be a right of action, and a further number clearly don't think of seeing a solicitor about this."

> "There are still people who find solicitors frightening ... this scheme smooths the path for people with a minimum of exposure to solicitors."

There was a little evidence of the differing expectations of free interviews as between solicitors and clients hinted at in Chapter 3. While those clients who had been advised not to proceed with a claim at their free interview were often quite satisfied with the outcome and grateful for the chance to talk over the matter with a qualified person, this type of encounter did not always please solicitors:

> "This client merely wanted somebody to talk to and we do not believe he ever had any real intention of pressing a claim. In our opinion therefore this particular interview was a waste of time and effort."

In another case it transpired that the client had already instructed another firm of solicitors and was simply using the opportunity of the free interview scheme to obtain a 'second opinion'. Not surprisingly the solicitor granting the free interview was not pleased to discover this fact, and felt that some sort of safeguard against such practice might be introduced into the scheme.

There were, however, very few cases where the solicitor found cause to complain and this was reflected in their comments.

2 THE SCHEME

On balance most of the solicitors felt that the scheme was worthwhile from their point of view, although there were some reservations expressed:

> "The scheme can only be beneficial in the sense that it helps break down the fear that some people have of entering a solicitor's office. However, there is the disadvantage that it helps spread the unfortunate idea that every accident will merit compensation regardless of whether there has been negligence or of whose fault the negligence was."

> "We think the scheme a good one but, to be fair, we have had no 'lemons' so far."

Several solicitors saw the scheme as being valuable not only in so far as it assisted accident victims to obtain compensation, but from their own point of view, as a useful source of contacts:

> "If I successfully settle a personal injury action for a client using the coupon scheme then if he wants a will drawn up or wants to sell his house he will come back to me rather than going elsewhere."

The solicitors felt that the work was no more or less lucrative than the other personal injury actions which they dealt with and, with very few exceptions, were happy to continue arranging free interviews with accident victims who had sent in coupons.

6

Summary and Conclusion

This study has attempted to evaluate a practical scheme designed to improve knowledge about claiming compensation for personal injury and to remove some of the barriers which seem to prevent accident victims from obtaining legal advice. The study has focussed on (1) the characteristics of the people using the scheme in relation to available evidence on use of legal services by accident victims; (2) the outcome of free interviews granted under the scheme; and (3) the subjective views of users and solicitors involved in the scheme. Some of the main findings are as follows:

1. Certain groups of accident victims which had previously been seen to have a low propensity to seek legal advice after an accident, were found to be using the free interview scheme in higher proportions than might be expected in normal circumstances. These were specifically, women; the elderly; and people not in full-time employment.

2. The highest proportion of scheme users were people who had suffered accidents *other* than on the road or at work. In the National Compensation Survey this group of accident victims was by far the *least* likely to seek legal advice after an accident.

3. The injuries suffered by scheme users were often serious. Some 10 per cent had suffered serious *permanent* disability and a further 17 per cent were still suffering serious residual effects of injuries from which complete recovery was uncertain.

4. Forty-two per cent of people using the scheme claimed that they had *not* thought about the possibility of trying to get compensation before they saw a leaflet or poster advertising the scheme.

5. Nearly two-thirds of accident victims using the scheme had never consulted a solicitor before about any matter.

6. Eighty per cent of free interviews granted resulted in some action being taken by solicitors to obtain compensation.

7. By the end of the study period 42 per cent of claims taken up had been settled and a further 41 per cent were still being negotiated. A total of £136,742 had been obtained in settlements, with an average settlement of £1,210 (median settlement of £600).

8. Users of the scheme were in general most satisfied with the advice they had received through the scheme and the handling of claims. There were, however, a number of complaints of poor advice, lack of interest and inefficiency on the part of some solicitors.

9. Users' views as to the value of the scheme indicated that the offer of a *free* initial interview was probably the most important feature of the scheme, particularly since so few people were aware of the existence of Legal Aid. There was also considerable evidence that the availability of leaflets acted as a stimulus to the idea of claiming compensation and reduced apprehension and confusion about how to proceed with a claim for damages.

In broad terms the accident leaflet scheme represents a highly economical method of providing information to accident victims about claiming compensation for their injuries, together with a positive incentive to take some action. It seems likely on the evidence of this study that the majority of those using the scheme *would not* have attempted to make a claim for damages had it not been for the scheme's existence. In the light of the reports of losses sustained and suffering endured by accident victims this must be interpreted as a positive finding.

If the scheme is to continue and its effectiveness to be increased, greater co-operation is necessary from hospitals in particular to ensure that adequate supplies of leaflets and posters are maintained, since these are the most obvious points of contact. Indeed, as many accident victims themselves suggested, the scheme would benefit from more publicity generally.

Appendix 1. Response rates

PATTERN OF RESPONSE TO POSTAL QUESTIONNAIRE

Figure 7.1 indicates the pattern of returns over the survey period. Following the initial mailing 226 questionnaires were received in the first two-and-a-half weeks period. This represents 47 per cent of the number initially mailed and 56 per cent of the total finally returned. Following the first reminder, a further 111 were received representing 23 per cent of the number originally mailed and a further 31 per cent of the total received. After the final reminder a final 79 questionnaires were received which represents 16 per cent of the total number of questionnaires originally mailed and 10 per cent of all those questionnaires returned. Figure 7.1 shows that of the 483 questionnaires mailed, 47 per cent were returned within two weeks; 70 per cent within 5 weeks and 86 per cent were returned by 11 weeks after the initial mailing.

ANALYSIS OF NON-RESPONDENTS

A limited analysis of non-respondents to the postal questionnaire indicated that women were significantly more likely to return questionnaires than men.

Table 7.1. Response to the postal questionnaire in relation to sex of scheme user.[1]

	Men	Women	All
	No.	No.	No.
Respondents	178	205	383
Non-respondents	45	17	62
Total	223	222	445

NOTE:
1. Figures are given where sex was known
2. $\chi^2 = 15$, df $= 1$, $p < \cdot 001$

Figure 7.1. Response to postal questionnaire over survey period.

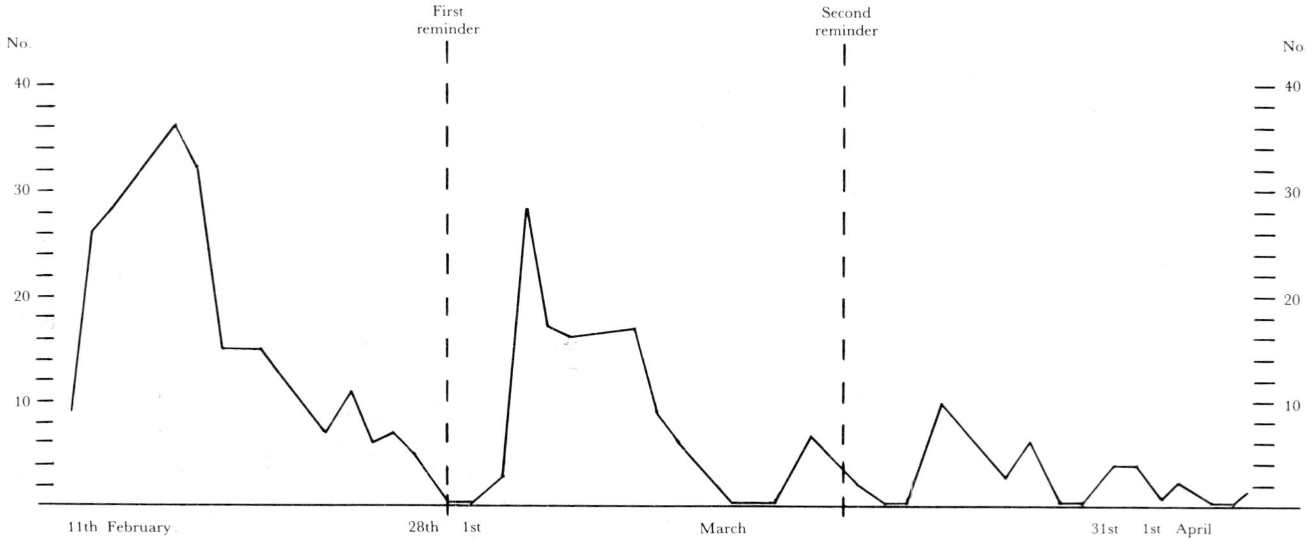

In addition to the information which was available about non-respondents from the coupons, it was also possible to look at non-response in relation to the outcome of interviews with solicitors. This was achieved by including non-respondents in the brief questionnaires sent to solicitors. Since these questionnaires were designed principally to obtain information about the outcome of claims being negotiated on behalf of those people who had *responded* to the postal questionnaire, we did not gather any extra information about non-respondents. However from these questionnaires to solicitors information about the outcome of interviews with solicitors was obtained for 51 of the 66 non-respondents. Of these non-respondents 7 (14 per cent) had failed

In addition to the information which was available about non-respondents from the coupons, it was also possible to look at non-response in relation to the outcome of interviews with solicitors. This was achieved by including non-respondents in the brief questionnaires sent to solicitors. Since these questionnaires were designed principally to obtain information about the outcome of claims being negotiated on behalf of those people who had *responded* to the postal questionnaire, we did not gather any extra information about non-respondents. However from these questionnaires to solicitors information about the outcome of interviews with solicitors was obtained for 51 of the 66 non-respondents. Of these non-respondents 7 (14 per cent) had failed to attend the free interview which had been arranged for them. One case was apparently not an accident and would therefore have been excluded from the survey in any case. A further 8 respondents (16 per cent) had been advised not to proceed with a claim and the remaining 35 cases were advised to proceed. Of this number 12 (34 per cent) had been settled by solicitors; 11 cases (31 per cent) were still being negotiated and 12 claims (34 per cent) had apparently been abandoned. Of the 12 claims that had been settled the amount of settlement was known in 11 cases and are as follows:

£ 25	£ 575
£ 80	£ 650
£ 250	£ 700
£ 350	£1,125
£ 400	£9,000
£ 400	

Although the figure for abandoned claims is considerably higher among non-respondents than among respondents (*cf.* Table 3.3) it may be a little misleading since it is possible that solicitors may have indicated that a claim was abandoned when in fact no action had been taken. Throughout this study a distinction has been drawn between cases in which the outcome of the free interview was advice not to proceed with a claim ('no claim') and cases where the decision not to proceed any further is made after some action has in fact been taken to initiate proceedings. This distinction may not have been clear on the questionnaire to solicitors and hence certain cases may be classified as 'abandoned' when in fact no action had been taken.

In any event the information on outcome of interviews among non-respondents to the postal questionnaire suggests that they are sufficiently in keeping with the proportions of respondents succeeding with claims not to affect the validity of the findings of the postal questionnaire dramatically. If the figures for non-respondents are combined with those for respondents, the percentage difference for outcome of claims is not altered by more than 2 per cent in any category (*cf.* Table 3.3).

Appendix 2

The Postal Questionnaire to Scheme Users

ERIC KNOTT
Solicitor
Liaison Officer and
Secretary to the Legal Services Committee

The Law Society
Greater Manchester Legal Services Committee
Pall Mall Court
67 King Street
Manchester M60 9AX
Telephone 061-832 7112

In any reply please quote

Your reference
Date

Last year you sent us a coupon requesting a free interview with a solicitor to discuss an accident claim. These coupons are part of a scheme which the Greater Manchester Legal Services Committee has organised to help accident victims obtain legal advice.

We are now hoping to improve and possibly extend this scheme and in order to do this it is very important for us to know about the experiences of those people who have used the scheme and about any suggestions they might have.

To help us in this we would be grateful if you would complete the enclosed questionnaire and return it to us in the stamped, addressed envelope provided. All of the information which you give is absolutely confidential and will not be linked with your name.

If you have any questions about the survey please contact myself or Mr. Eric Knott at the Law Society. The telephone number is 832 7112.

Thank you for your co-operation.

Yours sincerely,

Hazel G. Genn
Director of Research

Ref: □□□□□□□□□□□

1–11

Greater Manchester Legal Services Committee

Solicitors Free Interview Scheme

Questionnaire to Users

These first questions are to let us know about the type of accident which you had and what sort of injuries you suffered.

OFFICE USE ONLY COLUMN

Q1(a) Where did your accident take place and how did it happen?

(Please describe as fully as you can)

☐ 12
☐ 13
☐ 14
☐ 15

(b) What injuries did you suffer in the accident?

(Please describe as fully as you can)

☐ 16
☐ 17

(c) When did your accident happen?

(Please write in month and year)

Month	Year

☐☐ 18 19
☐☐ 20 21

(d) For how long were you ill after your accident?

(Please tick the appropriate box)

- Less than 1 week ☐
- 1 or 2 weeks ☐
- 3 or 4 weeks ☐
- 5 or 6 weeks ☐
- 7 or 8 weeks ☐
- More than 2months ☐

☐ 22

(e) Are you still affected by your injuries? If so please say in what way you are affected.

(Please describe how affected)

☐☐ 23 24

These questions are to let us know how you found out about the free interview scheme and whether you had thought about trying to claim compensation BEFORE you saw the leaflet.	*OFFICE USE ONLY COLUMN*
Q2(a) Where did you find out about the free interview scheme? *(Please say WHERE you heard about it and GIVE NAME of hospital, doctor's surgery, Citizen's Advice Bureau etc)*	25 ☐
(b) Did you find out about the scheme by seeing a poster; seeing a leaflet; somebody in the hospital telling you about it; or some other way? *(Tick the appropriate boxes)* Saw poster ☐ Saw leaflet ☐ Someone in hospital told me ☐ Other way *(Describe)* ☐	☐☐ 26–27
(c) When you sent in your coupon **who** did you think you might be able to claim compensation from? *(Please say from whom, e.g. employer, other driver, neighbour, council, manufacturer etc)*	☐ 28
(d) Why did you think that you might be able to claim compensation from them? *(Please give your reasons as fully as you can)*	☐☐ 29–30
(e) Had you thought about trying to get some compensation **before** you saw or heard of the leaflet? *(Please tick appropriate box)* Yes ☐ No ☐	☐ 31
If **"yes"** – What had you thought about?	☐☐ 32–33

These questions are about what happened when you went for your free interview with the solicitor

OFFICE USE ONLY COLUMN

Q3(a) When you went to see the solicitor what did he advise you to do and what reasons did he give you for his advice?

(Please describe the advice and reasons as fully as you can)

34–35

(b) What did you **think** about what the solicitor advised you to do? Were you **satisfied** with what he said?

(Please say what you thought — whether or not you were happy with the advice)

36–37

(c) Had you ever been to see a solicitor before — about any matter?

(Please tick appropriate box)

Yes ☐
No ☐
Can't remember ☐

38

Q4(a) IF THE SOLICITOR ADVISED YOU TO MAKE A CLAIM:

What is the position of the claim now?

(Please tick the appropriate box)

Claim settled ☐
Claim not yet settled ☐
Claim abandoned ☐
Don't know position ☐

39

*If claim has been SETTLED please state for how much: £*________

40–41

(b) Who did you make a claim against?

(Please state person e.g. employer, other driver, neighbour etc.)

42–43

So that we can tell how the scheme is working for all groups of people, these next questions ask for some details about yourself

OFFICE USE ONLY COLUMN

Q5(a) Are you:

(Please tick)

Male ☐
Female ☐

44

(b) Are you:

(Please tick)

Single ☐
Married ☐
Separated/Divorced ☐
Widowed ☐

45

(c) Are you:

(Please tick)

Employed Full-time ☐
Employed Part-time ☐
Housewife fulltime ☐
Unemployed ☐
Student ☐
Retired ☐
Off work sick/Disabled ☐

46

(d) What is your age? ☐

47

(e) What kind of work do you do **OR** what was your last main paid job?

(Please state kind of work as fully as you can)

48–49

(f) What kind of work does your husband/wife do OR what was their last main paid job?

(Please state the kind of work they do or DID as fully as you can)

50

OFFICE USE ONLY COLUMN

These last questions are for your comments about the scheme in general to help us to improve it and to extend it

Q6 Please state what you think about the free interview scheme for people who have had accidents and in what ways it helped you personally

☐ 51
☐ 52
☐ 53

Q7 Do you think that you would have gone to see a solicitor about claiming compensation if you **HAD NOT** used the scheme?

☐ 54
☐ 55
☐ 56

☐☐ 57 58
☐☐ 59 60
☐☐ 61 62
☐☐ 63 64

Thank you for completing this questionnaire

We hope that your answers will help us to make legal services more easily available

P.T.O.

Appendix 3

The Accident Leaflet

Coupon

I should like to have a free interview about an accident claim.
Please arrange an appointment for me with a solicitor near my home or work address. (Put down the address which suits you best.)

My name is

My home address is

Please send this coupon to:
Liaison Officer,
Legal Services Committee,
The Law Society,
Pall Mall Court,
67 King Street,
Manchester M60 9AX

Coupon address:
Liaison Officer,
Legal Services Committee,
The Law Society,
Pall Mall Court,
67 King Street,
Manchester M60 9AX
Tel: 061-832 7112

Prepared by the Lord Chancellor's Office and the Greater Manchester Legal Services Committee and the Central Office of Information 1981
Printed in England for Her Majesty's Stationery Office by Fellgrove Printers Ltd. Dd. 8202653 Pro 15814

Accidents can happen!

Get legal help if it happens to you

- Legal Aid can give you a solicitor's help at low cost or no cost
- FREE interview
- This leaflet tells you more

Legal Aid

Accidents can happen!

- At work
- Out shopping
- In the home
- On the roads . . . if you are a driver, passenger, or pedestrian – or if you just trip over a paving stone

Is someone else to blame?

It could be –

- Your employer
- A workmate
- Another driver
- Your landlord
- The council
- A shopkeeper or
- A seller of faulty goods

Can I get compensation?

If someone else is to blame, you may get compensation for your injuries, loss of wages, damage to clothing and so on.

A solicitor can advise you whether you have a good case.

Legal Aid

How do I get advice?

Here are a few ways of getting legal advice. Choose the one that suits you best.

- See your solicitor
- If you don't have a solicitor, fill in the coupon on the back of this leaflet for a FREE INTERVIEW with a solicitor. Send it to the address on the coupon. A solicitor will then write to you and suggest an appointment
- If you have had an accident at work, your trade union official may be able to advise you
- Go to your local Citizens Advice Bureau. (The address is in the phone book.) Or go to another local Advice Centre
- If you are kept in hospital, ask to see the Medical Social Worker

What will it cost me?

If you send off the coupon, your first interview with a solicitor will be free. The solicitor will tell you if you can get Legal Aid.

With Legal Aid, a solicitor's help need not be expensive. Many people pay nothing at all for Legal Aid. Whether you get it depends on your income and savings.

Legal Aid